PREGNANT MOMENTS

Rebirthing Life to Situations

Written by Katrina Carmichael

Inspired by My Sister Circle

Copyright © 2014 Katrina Carmichael

All rights reserved. No part of this book may be reproduced in any form or by any means, electronic or mechanical, including photo-copying, recording, or by any information storage and retrieval system, without written permission from the author. This excludes a reviewer who may quote brief passages in a review. Unless otherwise noted, all Scripture quotations are from The Holy Bible, King James Version (KJV)

Published by G Publishing, LLC

ISBN: 978-0-9883374-9-7

Printed in the United States of America

PREGNANT MOMENTS

Rebirthing Life to Situations

This book is dedicated to the memory of my beloved sister, Michelle Carmichael-Walker and to all my sisters across the world!

Love is a beautiful thing...
why not start it with you!

"Ye are the light of the world. A city that is set on an hill cannot be hid. ...Let your light so shine before men, that that they may see your good works, and glorify your Father which is in heaven."
Matthew 5:14,16

(All Biblical quotations are from the King James version unless otherwise marked.)

By my Sister Friend,

Shirley Phillips

Foreword:
"My Sister Circle"

The ONLY. I always prided myself on being the ONLY child. I got the ONLY toys, the only clothes, the ONLY hugs, and the only kisses in my single-parent (ONLY) home. Siblings were not on my Christmas list, and I did not envy any of my friends with homes inundated with obnoxious sisters and brothers. You see, I loved the attention I received from my mother, and I basked in the glory of being her one and ONLY. My mother WAS my sister, my brother, my father, and my best friend. However, as an adult, suffering the loss of my mother in 2005, the ONLY me soon became the LONELY me. Up until that point, I always believed the old adage "you can't miss it if you've never had it." But I did miss "it." And I had to have "it." In fact, my very life depended on this "it." The "it" was the embodiment of a sister. Not just one, but a full circle of them.

Family is not always born of blood. I've had "family" who knew I was starving yet offered nothing to eat. I've had "family" who laughed as I stared in the face of eviction. I've had "family" who I wouldn't wish on my worst enemy. Some of the most hurtful comments and offenses to ever be directed at me have come from (you guessed it) family. My girlfriends (or "sisterfriends," as I affectionately call them) have proven time and time again that for "only children" like me, blood is not always thicker than water. These women have been there for me unceasingly, almost instinctively. They have proven that sisterhood is *earned*, not inherited. My sisters have not only helped me through the death of my mother but also through the nasty breakups, the smoking-hot hook-ups, the self-hate, the layoffs, the empty bank accounts, the promotions at work, the pregnancies, the new beginnings, and the fateful endings. Most importantly, they helped me face my worst enemy, who was none other than…well…me. When I was downtrodden and devoid of hope, my sisters got in the trenches and went to work on the restoration of me. The ONLY me.

My sister circle is not limited to mere gossiping, shopping, and sharing Carrie Bradshaw-esque relationship tidbits. It's a collectively diversified triage of like-minded women helping one another be comfortable with the ugly side of ourselves we try to mask from the world. It is not only about interacting with my peers and colleagues but also about embracing the elder women of wisdom in my life who have walked my path and have made my mistakes, like a professor, a hair stylist, a pastor, even a boss. Most importantly, those I call "sister" are willing to add to and fortify our circle, not just take from it. This phenomenal female presence of women is about uplifting and sometimes even knocking each other off of our high pedestals when we are inflated by delusions of grandeur and pretention. This fortress has helped me face reality, adversity, and has most recently taught me the difference between tough love and deliberate abuse. Unlike many so-called sister circles, our driving force is admiration and respect rather than its ugly underside, whose names are envy and loathing.

Every woman needs a reliable hand-picked circle of sisters. The circle keeps us grounded and in touch with our inner selves. It also gives us a shelter when we are discarded and cast aside by the men in our lives or even by society as a whole. My circle of sisters has engulfed me and shaded me from the storm when the rest of the world has given up. It has been my mother, my father, and, in some cases, my significant other. Watching the ball drop on New Year's Eve, a tissue in Church after the pastor's message spoke directly to me, chocolate-covered strawberry treats on February 14th, a card received in the mail "just because," a stern reminder of why I should never "recycle" a boyfriend: all jewels given to me by my sisters.

This circle inspires me to remain perpetually uncomfortable with the status quo in order to institute change within the world I live. It reminds me to never forsake the dreams I had at 12, but to also dream even bigger at 37. A true sister circle should never be confused with a clique, as cliques are closed and unwelcoming. Our circle may be extended, but we are ever so cautious as to who may be inducted in. Just as a wolf attempts to infiltrate a flock of sheep, some women attempt to masquerade as "sisters"—which is quite possibly why so many women find it virtually impossible to interact and connect with others like themselves.

All in all, I can proudly say I am no longer an "only". I am a sister, and to my sisters I will forever be grateful.

Acknowledgments

I want to give honor to God who is my Alpha and Omega, recognizing that I am the Head and not the Tail. I thank the Lord for my gift of expression through words. I thank my Sister Circle: My momma, my sisters Michelle and Tammy, my niece Mia, my publisher Ms. Julia Hunter, Shirley, Mechelle, Sandy, Nichole, Andreatta (Pookie), Briana, Deb, Ashanti, Tina, Nita, Kiwi, Mikki, Sonya, Shana, Nikiya, Nicole, Brenda, Sharon, Edith, Lisa, Karen and a host of many others for all of your love and support!

GONE, BUT NEVER FORGOTTEN

Michelle Carmichael-Walker
January 23, 1974-May 20, 2003

Inside the Minds of Every Woman

My Introduction — Sister2Sister

> *"I will praise thee; for I am fearfully and wonderfully made: marvelous are thy works; and that my soul knoweth right well." Psalm 139:14*

Every woman wants to be loved. Every woman wants to be acknowledged and respected in her relationships. Women also want to know that their partner always has their best interest at heart. When a woman walks into a room, either with or without her mate, there should be no misunderstanding, whether he walks in with her or is already in the room, that they are truly an item. Their status as a couple can be indicated with a simple kiss on the forehead, hand holding, eye contact, or a really delicate embrace.

Women also want stability. Even though, in many instances, women can provide for themselves, they still like to know that their mate would be able to carry the weight on his own for a while if something came up, such as a child birth, career change, or layoff. A good friend of mine once told me, "You can't build a castle on sand." Overall, women are not complicated creatures, but the world they live in definitely is!

A woman can have many girlfriends, but only true friends stay around. True friends don't judge you. They are with you during the good and bad times. They love you with all of your faults. You can travel with them, disagree with them, have fellowship with them, and pray with them. They are your GOD-sent sisters.

True friends share a sacred circle. The sacred circle does not admit what I call the 3 M's. We don't share men, money, or our mouths. True friends don't date the men you've dated, don't borrow money (or only in desperate times of need), and don't discuss each other's business outside the circle. True friends normally don't have to discuss the rules of the sacred circle; they're a given!

Of course, we need to take time out to get to know ourselves FIRST before we enter into relationships.

We need to set up our own Bill of Rights about what we will and will not accept in relationships. We then need to start dating JACK and not the BOX. Just because the outside looks good, that doesn't mean it's good for you. Get to know a person's inner spirit. Even though, we can never get to know an individual totally, we need to stop ignoring red flags in the beginning of relationships: how he acts under pressure, how he treats an individual (stranger) who he feels can do nothing to or for him (i.e., a waitress, drive-thru worker, peddler). These things determine character. We then need to start honoring the covenant of relationships, especially marriages. No one respects relationships anymore. A man can't cheat by himself.

So, the best advice that I can give, sister to sister, is to make the best of what you have; stop looking for someone to define or complete you; define yourself so that he can get to know you and what you like and don't like, what makes you happy, what moves you, what tickles your fancy, what you will and will not accept, and so on and so on, sista! First and foremost, love yourself, put GOD first in your life, and I promise you that everything else will fall in its place!

Contents

Foreword: 5
Acknowledgments 10
My Introduction—Sister2Sister 13
THE DARK SIDE OF DATING 19

Section 1: EYES WIDE OPEN SHUT!

Eyes Wide Open Shut! 21
I Remember… 25
The Break-Up 29
Love Shouldn't Hurt 31
Moment of Truth 35
Needful Things 38
Our Love…The Weathered Storm 42

Section 2: I AM FROM

I AM FROM 45
Innocent Child 47
Who am I? 49
My Mother's Strength 51
Unmasked 53
Trapped in a Box 55
Normalcy 57
S2S Promise 59

THE DARK SIDE OF DATING

Relationships and Domestic Violence

The way we can start acting and behaving differently in regards to domestic violence is by educating ourselves about the topic. Domestic violence in relationships stems from one member wanting control and power over the other. We need to learn how to resolve issues without violence. Our conflict-resolution skills stink to high heaven these days! We think that hitting or cursing out someone is the answer. The answer is to STOP, WALK AWAY, and COOL OFF!

Will domestic violence ever end? Probably not, but, because we now know what we know, it doesn't have to dwell in our house!

Section 1

<u>EYES WIDE OPEN SHUT!</u>

"My dear brothers and sisters, take note of this: Everyone should be quick to listen, slow to speak and slow to become angry." - James 1:19 (Holy Bible International Version, NIV)

On May 20, 2003, Michelle's life was taken away from her three beautiful children, her parents, her siblings, and a host of relatives and friends by her husband. One man changed the lives of so many. Even though Michelle's life was taken at the tender age of 29, Michelle's memory stays alive in those who were closest to her.

"The people that walked in darkness have seen a great light: they that dwell in the land of the shadow of death, upon them hath the light shined." Isaiah 9:2

No one truly understands why one abuses another, but there is no excuse for it. No one knows why a person stays in an abusive relationship, so let us not judge.

Let's take a walk on the dark side of dating. Keep your eyes open because sometimes, Our Eyes Are Wide Open... Shut!

Eyes Wide Open Shut!

Sometimes our eyes are wide open,
Yet we cannot see.
Let me give you a dose of Michelle's reality.

The simple fact
Was that he was not the right man for me.

Yet, I dealt with him
And all his inconsistencies.
And beat myself up
Because he turned out not to be
The man he said he would be

The one that would be there for me

No matter what

I could be pretty enough,
smart enough,
sexy enough,
thin enough,
In his eyes
And then to my surprise
Not only did I become his punching bag
But I became an object
To release his stress onto
And then do whatever else
He wanted to do to me
and by the end of the night
He was apologizing to me
demonstrating how a true man's supposed to be.
I'm confused, frustrated, dazed, and in pain
For allowing myself to be taken advantage of
But that's what happens
When you don't know the true meaning of love.
My eyes were wide-open shut.

Trying to fill a void
A void that has left me feeling empty inside
Because I have been hiding, harboring
All the bitterness, the mistrust

And just the simple know-how
Of being loved all my life
Now what do you do
When you come to realize
That you are a beautiful woman
and that you will not comprise
Yourself for him or any other man
This is the day that you allow him to see and understand
His unkind and wicked ways
The years of agony and pain that he has dumped on you over the years,
letting him know
"I've cried my last tears."
You will no longer
Abuse me, offend me, judge me
I'm no longer your punching bag, nor your property.

My eyes are wide open
Now I see.
I see you for who you truly are
You're a coward, a buster…a sorry excuse for a man
Sorry, I had to interrupt your plans
To completely destroy me

My eyes are wide open

Now I see
My eyes are wide open
Now I see
I'm no longer blind, nor in bondage
Thank God you set me free!

"Set your affection on things above, not on things on the earth." Colossians 3:2

Do you remember the first time you laid eyes on the man who literally made you feel like the world had completely stopped? That man who made you feel you were the woman that GOD had finally sent to him. The man who vowed to love, protect, honor, and adore you? The man who made you feel "complete." The man who hung his player's jacket up, just for you? Now close your eyes and imagine never being able to see this person again…how do you feel? Imagine catching this person cheating on you…how do you feel? Imagine this person yelling at you, punching you, choking you, hurting you…now, how do you feel?
I Remember…

I Remember…

I Remember…
The first time we met
How our eyes connected
And how good it felt
As if there were no other
I'd met my friend, my soul mate, my lover

You hypnotized me with your kind words
You totally swept me off my feet
We talked for endless hours
About our childhood, our jobs, our future
And even when our parents would meet

I Remember…
How you used to just hold me
And how you used to tell me how much you loved me.
How it left butterflies all up in my stomach
How there was no one after me
How we walked closely
hand in hand
Watching the waves of the sea

I Remember…

When I said, "I do."
How you vowed to love me as Christ loved the church.
How happy we were after our first child's birth.

I Remember…
The first day you played Dr. Jackal and Mr. Hyde.
How you cursed me out, choked me up,
And how my body did the electric slide
Across the room onto our bed

I never expected to feel this sad
Broken, hurt, and embarrassed
By the man that you've become
I blame myself for being so dumb.

I Remember…
When I took my vows it was for better or for worse.
But I didn't know that involved being abused
And mistreated
God help me, please…
I feel as if I'm a prisoner in my own home
Up under a curse.

I Remember…

How I was before we met
How I use to just love me
And how good it felt
Not to be afraid to just be me,
Happy-go-lucky, independent, and free

Oh, how I remember…
The day that I tried to leave
How you harassed me, stalked me, tormented me,
Every second of the day
It was as if you were on a mission
Letting nothing stand nor get in your way.
I Remember…I Remember…

How I prayed to my GOD
to make this and you just go away
Why me, Lord? I'm a good person,
I prided myself on walking right and tried to obey.

I remember…my my my…my GOD's reply,
"Dear Child, It was time to have you by my side."

I Remember…

"For with God nothing shall be impossible."
Luke 1:37

Last night I had an epiphany! I made up in my mind that I wanted a new lease on life. I wanted to start living and not just going with the flow. I wanted to experience some normalcy in my life. I'd hit my rock bottom. I wanted to LEARN how to love myself. I kept hearing, "I CAN DO BAD BY MYSELF." I wanted to be set free.
This led to the Break-Up!

The Break-Up

I woke up this morning with a new lease on life.
I broke up with my boyfriend last night.

I told him that it was time for me to love *me*.
I didn't fear him anymore.
I was tired; I wanted to be set free.
I didn't care about him banging on my door in the middle of the night,
Coming up to my job intimidating me, wanting to fight.
I broke up with my boyfriend last night.
I couldn't take any more of his abuse.
I was tired of running from the simple truth.

He was not the right man for me,
Because I know that this is not what God had
    intended for me.
It had got to the point where I couldn't even count
    the number of incidents there had been
Or how many more there were to come.

I broke up with my boyfriend last night.

He begged for me to take him back.
"I'm a changed man, I'm ready to make it all right."
I wanted to believe him.
I wanted him back…
Then I thought about my sister, my deceased sister.
I could hear her literally whispering in my ear.
I broke up with my boyfriend last night.

There's no turning back.
God's going to mend these broken pieces and
    prepare me for the next man in my life.

But I can't worry about that right now…
Today I'm free.
I broke up with my boyfriend last night.

"And now these three remain: faith, hope and love. But the greatest of these is love." I Corinthians 13:13 (Holy Bible International Version, NIV)

Love is not perfect, and you definitely cannot enter a relationship presuming that everything will be. Love is kind; love is gentle; love is peaceful; love is free; and love is like the wind. Love is GOD; you can't see him, but you can feel him…LOVE shouldn't hurt!

Love Shouldn't Hurt

I wish I would've known from the start…
I would've ended it.
I wish I would've known he was not right for me.
But you know how it is in the beginning…
You see no wrong.

Love shouldn't be this hard.

But now my heart is heavy, hurt,
My spirit is broken.
The man who once spoke nothing but kind words to
    me…treated me like I was his world,
Is now a mere image, a cloudy vision, a piece of my
    history.

I'm so mad at what he has done to me.
Yet, I allowed it to happen,
Hence the IRONY!
He lied to me, he deceived me.
This man even CHEATED on me.
He cheated me out of my happiness, my time.
He cheated me out of normalcy.

He left me with more than what I even started the relationship with…BAGGAGE!
Heavy bags, sometimes too heavy to carry.
He took me on a ride, a journey, a trip.
He took me on the dark side of dating.

Whatever he needed and if I was able to give,
He had it!
What was mine, was his.
I accepted everything from him,
But he took everything from me.
He took my sense of pride, my self-esteem, my happiness.
He broke my spirit.
He took the ability for me to just love me.
He left me feeling like a bag of broken bones.
I didn't know what to do.
So I ran…
I ran to the one place that I knew I would be safe.
I ran…

I ran...
I ran to God.
I ran without looking back…
I ran fast…
I ran faster
  and I started dropping bags
  heavy bags, pain-filled bags, bitter bags,
    resentment bags, not-loving me bags.

And this is when the healing started.

GOD mended these broken bones.
He put them back in place.
He renewed a spirit within me.
I'm at peace.
I've been saved by his endless mercy and grace.

"For thy lovingkindness is before mine eyes: and I have walked in thy truth." Psalm 26:3

Ladies, we need to stop being dumping yards, welcome-home mats, and parking lots to the men in our lives. We enable men to do what they do to us. A man can only do what you allow him to.

Always express yourself in a relationship. Neither men nor women are mind readers. Like grandma used to say, "Say what you mean; mean what you say." As enablers, we allow men to abuse us, tear down our self-esteem, and deprive us of being who we truly are and of what we really want to do. We women get so caught up in needing someone in our lives when, in actuality, we are trying to fill a void that only we can fill. We just want to be loved, but allowing different spirits to dwell in you is not the way.

Ladies, stop standing in your own way. Sometimes I have to minister to myself! I don't know everything about relationships, but I've been in enough to know what I know.

Here is my Moment of Truth.

Moment of Truth

I think I gave into you
Too fast
Too freely
Too willingly
To just be disappointed again
Why do I keep allowing myself
To be a dumping yard, a parking lot,
A welcome-home mat
To these insignificant men?

Without thinking about what tomorrow would bring
I feel as if I should have just waited,
But guess what,
It's too late.
There's no time to contemplate
No room to debate
On what should've and could've been done.
Because that was yesterday.
Today is today.

Will you respect me and think I am
As beautiful as I was to you that first day?
Do you still want to spend time with me,
Get to know me in the most intimate ways?
Or am I just that booty call, your little freak, that
     quick lay?
I can't be mad at no one but me

Yet as pretentious as it must be
For me to be loved so easily, yet give myself up so freely.
As if I didn't love myself
To take a chance with a man
Who doesn't even give me a second glance.
Just some idle chit-chat over the phone.
What do you expect when you've already given the dog its bone.
The cat-and-mouse chase,
Game is over!
There goes, there went…*poof* my four-leaf clover.

Bad luck and men my middle name
Not to mention the agony and pain
I've caused myself time and time again.
Sometimes it feels like a Category 3 whirlwind.

My body is my house
I own it
I make the payment and have insurance on it
I keep it up
It's my fault that I leased it out.
To another undeserving man
I need to stop
Lord…this is becoming a trend.

Life can sometimes feel like a Category 3
    Whirlwind.
Destroying, Misplacing, Rearranging, and
    separating myself from self
Just having to start my life all over again

Life can sometimes feel like a Category 3 Hurricane
    Katrina Whirlwind,

This is my moment of truth!

"For God hath not given us the spirit of fear; but of power, and of love, and of a sound mind."
2 Timothy 1:7

In this day and age, having a successful relationship is very hard. No one really respects "relationships/marriages" anymore. They no longer honor the "covenant" of marriage. One of the main reasons is because people enter relationships for the wrong reasons. Just because it looks good doesn't necessarily mean it is good for you! Stop dating the box and start dating JACK, Do…da…do…da…dodododo, pops goes the weasel…start dating him, Boo! A lot of times we get what we want, not what we need…Needful Things!

Needful Things

Last night was another night
That I felt down and deprived
Deprived of things
Needful to me
Deprived of my love, safety, compassion, security, my soul mate, my MAN.

Just sympathetically speaking…

You cared no way or another
About how I truly felt
Because when I tried to talk to you
You stared at me, you glared at me,
You rolled your eyes, you turned your back and left.
I ask myself constantly, where is the
    communication?
Because without that…
We're like a recipe without the ingredients

Needful things

Yesterday
Was another day
That I felt down and deprived
Deprived of things needful to me

Deprived of my dream house
My dream boat
My stocks, my bonds
My wealth, my growth

Just sympathetically speaking!

Now what do I do,
When I have someone like you?
Who cares nothing about how our future looks
All you do is care about you

And how long it took you to make me
a part of your dreams
a team, please…by no means

Needful things

Today was another day that I felt down and
    deprived
Deprived of things needful to me
Deprived of all things that I was seeking out to be
Today was the day
That I changed his plans to my plans
Placed all fault in his hands
For depriving me
of not being…
Woman enough
Strong enough
Brave enough
Courageous enough
Daring enough
Willing enough
Loving and respecting myself enough

Let me catch my breath…

Today was the day
That I changed his plans to my plans
Placed all fault in his hands

For depriving me
of not being
Woman enough
Strong enough
Brave enough
Courageous enough
Daring enough
Willing enough
Loving and respecting myself enough

To leave his behind

Now who's looking, glaring, and staring at my picture
Wondering, why, oh why
You let something so special pass you by

Today was the day that I made a stand
Today was the day that I made a stand
Placed GOD's hand in my hand
made him as my man…AMEN…Peace

"Beareth all things, believeth all things, hopeth all things, endureth all things." I Corinthians 13:7

How many times have you been in a relationship that didn't work out or in a failed marriage that led to divorce?

Love is a beautiful thing when it is shared between two individuals who both have each other's interest at heart. True love lingers even when the road gets bumpy, when the arguments don't cease, and even when you have to separate yourselves from each other to gain peace of mind. Love weathers the storms.

Our Love…The Weathered Storm

As I look over the past several months that we have shared together
I think about all of the times that you've made them better
First by understanding my complaints
By acknowledging your mistakes
And wanting to move on
I thank the Lord for allowing us to weather the storm.

I not only appreciate you for understanding

But I appreciate you for putting up with me
Yes me, and my crazy and picky ways
I know I've had my share of days
Days of driving you insane
But again you weathered the storm
I know I am a rare form, a jewel…your priceless pearl.
Overall I'm just simply your girl!

I'm the Bonnie to your Clyde!
The Michelle to your Obama!
That suit to your tie.
I'm that ride-or-die chick
Who's got your back
Your biggest fan.
And as a matter of fact
My love for you leaves no gray areas at all.
It's beautiful like the Niagara Falls.

I love you through and through
I can see myself saying…
I do
One day to you and only you.
I know that day is soon to come,
But until then,
Let's celebrate our love
And pray that it continues to grow…our love, the weathered storm!

Section 2

I AM FROM

"Don't you know that you yourselves are God's temple and that God's Spirit dwells in your midst? – II Corinthians 3:16 (Holy Bible International Version, NIV)

This section is dedicated to those who were lost, yet now found; broken, but now healed; defeated, but now victorious. We need to start living our lives to our fullest potential, celebrating all life moments…good or bad. Everyone has a story. Your story may not be my story, but our stories are our TESTIMONIES! They shape and define our character. They allow others to see where we come from.

"My words shall be of the uprightness of my heart: and my lips shall utter knowledge clearly." Job 33:3

Do you know where you are from because if you don't, you will not know where you are going? I AM FROM…

I AM FROM

I AM FROM the 70s.
I AM FROM Verna Mae and CJ.
I AM FROM rowed houses paved in brick,
No backyard, no pool to play in, cockroaches and rodents.
I AM FROM gang violence to selling nickel and dime bags on the street.
I AM FROM claiming VICTORY over defeat.
I AM FROM the happiest day, when my son was born,
To the saddest day, when my sister died…rather murdered.
I AM FROM hurt and pain,
Broken dreams, broken promises.
I AM FROM old to new,
Recycling life situations all over again.
I AM FROM encouragement, success

Downfalls to failures.

I AM FROM GOD…
Who has mended these broken pieces when I felt torn and useless.
Who has kept me in the midst of my storm.

I AM FROM where trouble does not last long.
I AM FROM the Kingdom of Darkness
to the Kingdom of Light.
I AM FROM walking out of the spirit of fear, into the spirit of power.
I AM FROM CONFIDENCE.
I AM FROM KNOWLEDGE. *Faith*
I AM FROM FAITH.
I AM FROM a PRAYER WARRIOR.
I AM FROM HEALING.
I AM FROM the 70s.
I AM FROM Verna Mae and CJ.

"And, ye fathers, provoke not your children to wrath: but bring them up in the nurture and admonition of the Lord." Ephesians 6:4

Having a successful relationship requires work. Your relationship is your business, and you and your partner are the employees. If children are involved, they are your investments. In order for your business to operate successfully, you must come to work every day, pull your own weight, compromise, make sound business suggestions/decisions in the benefit of the company, and, overall, you must like what you do—if you catch my drift! Now, what do you do when the business goes out of business? How do you handle your investments…your innocent child?

Innocent Child

My son's father
Just up and left
Leaving me with a son
To take care of all by myself
Now who's going to help me
clothe and feed this son of mine
Because if you know what I know,

there sure ain't no daddies standing in line.
One day the bastard
May need his son
You never know when you have to come back
Paybacks are mean
And you reap what you sow
You may need your son
Who doesn't know
You from Adam
or any man on the street
You know when you left
That sure was deep
Forgive and turn the other cheek is the Christian
   way
Eat poop and die
Is sometimes what I want to say
This innocent child did nothing to you
Just needed a daddy
Who would love him
No matter what
His mom and dad went through.

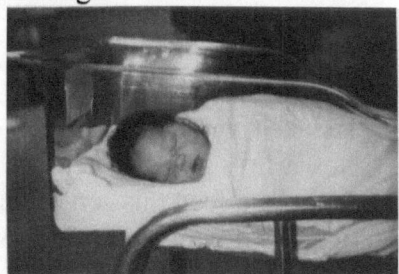

"So God created man in his own image..."
Genesis 1:27

Have you ever felt you really didn't know who you were, where you were going, what you were doing, or who you were doing it with? This is the most vulnerable time in a person's life. Before you can possibly allow yourself to be in a relationship, you must get to know yourself, what you like, what you don't like, what makes you happy, and what makes you tick. Ultimately, you must learn how to love yourself first and foremost. Now ask yourself, Who am I?

Who am I?

Who am I?
Am I being someone I'm not?
Am I living a life that I choose to live?
Or am I living a fairytale or a fib?
I ask myself, who am I?
The answer I get brings a tear to my eye.
I really don't know who I am.
It's like I am a movie star,
Living my life for my fans.
Am I supposed to change this attitude,
And give myself some self-esteem?

Maybe then I'll find out who I am,
And be the person I chose and want to be.
Who am I?

"Who can find a virtuous woman? for her price is far above rubies." Proverbs 31:10

Mothers are special people. A mother's love is unconditional. A mother is caring, nurturing, warm, considerate, and kind. A mother finds a way for her children. With God's assistance, a mother makes a way out of no way! A Mother's Strength is PRICELESS!

My Mother's Strength

As I look over the years
And look at the woman I've become
I think about my mother's love, strength, and warmth.
I think about how she kept us, molded us, and protected us
From hurt, harm, and deceit.
Barely having clothes on our back, shoes on our feet.
I remember how my mom would smile and watch us eat
Not knowing she did not have enough for herself
My mother's strength was definitely her wealth.

She laid the foundation for us to develop a
    relationship with God.
Having and maintaining a relationship with Christ
    made her proud
Even during what others would call our misery
My mom always seemed to muster up a smile,
    claiming VICTORY over DEFEAT!
Not only is she a survivor and burdened by the
    death of a child
She's motherless and fatherless, but she still stands
    proud!

My mother's strength and love,
Is unconditional, recyclable, organic
It beats to the sound of its own drums
It never ends as the world turns.

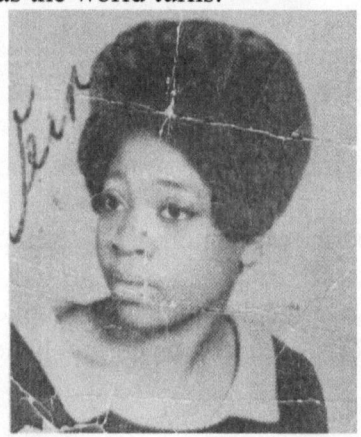

"Nothing in all creation is hidden from God's sight. Everything is uncovered and laid bare before the eyes of him to whom we must give account." Hebrews 4:13 (Holy Bible International Version, NIV).

When you look at me… what do you see?

Unmasked

Are you beautiful on the outside?
But scared of what others would think of you after knowing who you truly are,

what you've been through,
where you've been,
who you've been with,
and maybe the company you've kept?

Are you just going day by day hoping that no one will ever unveil the mask and find out the truth?

You feel as if you're living with the Achilles Syndrome…waiting to unveil the truth: your immortality, your low self-esteem, your lack of faith, your lose sense of hope.

You're not perfect, yet everyone thinks you are.

Everyone thinks you're great,
But YOU feel like a grasshopper amongst
 GIANTS!
Are you ready to shout out to the world and tell the
 world who you really are?

Are you ready to become UNMASKED!

"The Spirit you received does not make you slaves, so that you live in fear again; rather, the Spirit you received brought about your adoption to sonship. And by him we cry, 'Abba, Father.'" Romans 8:15 (Holy Bible International Version, NIV)

Have you ever felt that you were losing your mind, that no one could possibly understand what you were going through? Have you ever felt…TRAPPED!

Trapped in a Box

Trapped in a box
Nowhere to run
Nowhere to hide
The only thing you keep seeing
Is the four corners on each side.

Your life becomes dark
In the midst of your storm.
Each day growing weary
Life becoming a chore.

Trapped in a box
Nowhere to run
Nowhere to hide

Scared to make a move
Due to all of the pain and fear inside.

If I move to the right.
If I move to the left,
If I turn all of the way around
I still feel trapped
Surrounded by white walls

Scared to make a decision
About what step to take next
Am I in a straight jacket?
With my arms strapped against my chest?
Or is it just my mind dancing…racing
Trying to buy time?

Trapped in a box
Nowhere to run
Nowhere to hide
Scared to make a move
Due to all of the pain and fear inside.

"Be careful for nothing; but in every thing by prayer and supplication with thanksgiving let your requests be made known unto God. And the peace of God, which passeth all understanding, shall keep your hearts and minds through Christ Jesus."
Phil 4:6-7

Is normal even possible in this world that we live in today?

Normalcy

What is normal in this day and age?
When our men sage their pants and walk around in braids.
Killing one another for no apparent reason at all.
Because one's sitting short and the other is standing tall.
Women hating on one another trying to constantly compete.
With silicone in their breasts and butts,
Botox and face-lifts and tummy tucks,
that's become part of the monthly bills.
You noticed I haven't even talked about these young baby mamas and baby daddies trying to raise these kids or better yet kids raising kids.
On their own agendas as a matter of fact,

Lacking respect for life, their elders, and selves alike.
Is normal being able to perpetrate who and what you're not?
Not being able to speak English, yet drive a very expensive car.
Dropping out of school as if it was the thing to do.
When 12 years of free education has become 12 years a slave. Showing a lack of appreciation for the roads our ancestors have paved.

Not planning for tomorrow…barely making it day to day.

What is normal in this day and age?

WAKE UP…it's time for CHANGE!

S2S Promise

**To my little sisters (Sister2Sister)
coming into your own…this is for you!**
Can't nobody love you, like YOU!

From one sister to another, this is our
PROMISE.

I am SOMEBODY.

I am BEAUTIFUL.

I will RESPECT myself at all times.

I will take ACCOUNTABILITY for my actions.

I will do what I am REQUIRED to do.

I am a YOUNG LADY.

And I will CONDUCT myself APPROPRIATELY.

I will become a BETTER ME!

Written and Inspired by Katrina Carmichael
©2005

*Speak IT, Seek IT, and PRAY it into
EXISTENCE!*